OFFBEAT SPORTS

BY JON MARTHALER

THE WILD WORLD OF SPORTS

SportsZone

An Imprint of Abdo Publishing
abdopublishing.com

abdopublishing.com

Published by Abdo Publishing, a division of ABDO, PO Box 398166, Minneapolis, Minnesota 55439.
Copyright © 2018 by Abdo Consulting Group, Inc. International copyrights reserved in all countries.
No part of this book may be reproduced in any form without written permission from the publisher.
SportsZone™ is a trademark and logo of Abdo Publishing.

Printed in the United States of America, North Mankato, Minnesota
102017
012018

THIS BOOK CONTAINS
RECYCLED MATERIALS

Cover Photos: Dawn Villella/AP Images, foreground; Phelan M. Ebenhack/AP Images, background
Interior Photos: Everett Collection/Shutterstock Images, 5; Mitrofanov Alexander/Shutterstock Images,
6; Shutterstock Images, 7, 13; Carlos Baez Castro/Notimex/Newscom, 8; Jaap Arriens/Nur Photo/Sipa/AP
Images, 10; Rodrigo Oropeza/Xinhua News Agency/Newscom, 11; Nicolas Armer/picture-alliance/dpa/
AP Images, 14; Tristan Reynaud/Sipa/AP Images, 17, 18; Wayne Parry/AP Images, 19; Kyodo/AP Images,
20; Ernst Peters/Lakeland Ledger/AP Images, 22; Carlos Osorio/AP Images, 23; Ray McManus/Sportsfile/
Getty Images, 24–25; Sportsfile/Getty Images, 26; Fiorigian Luigi/iStockphoto, 27; Peter Komka/MTI/AP
Images, 29; Sebastien Salom-Gomis/SIPA/AP Images, 30–31; Michael Probst/AP Images, 32; Bonnie G.
Vculek/Enid News & Eagle/AP Images, 33; Peter Steffen/picture-alliance/dpa/AP Images, 35; Chris
Dillmann/Vail Daily/AP Images, 36; Andres Garcia Martin/iStockphoto, 37; Mike D. Abell/iStockphoto,
38; People Images/iStockphoto, 40; Niall Carson/Press Association/PA Wire URN:32431647/AP Images,
41; Stacey Lauren-Kennedy/Daily Gazette/AP Images, 43; Niall Carson/Press Association/PA Wire
URN:20324039 /AP Images, 44; David Durochik/AP Images, 44–45

Editor: Meg Gaertner
Series Designer: Craig Hinton

Publisher's Cataloging-in-Publication Data

Names: Marthaler, Jon, author.
Title: Offbeat sports / by Jon Marthaler.
Description: Minneapolis, Minnesota : Abdo Publishing, 2018. | Series: The wild world of sports | Includes
    online resources and index.
Identifiers: LCCN 2017946935 | ISBN 9781532113666 (lib.bdg.) | ISBN 9781532152542 (ebook)
Subjects: LCSH: Sports--United States--History--Juvenile literature. | Sports--Miscellanea--Juvenile
    literature.
Classification: DDC 796--dc23
LC record available at https://lccn.loc.gov/2017946935

TABLE OF
CONTENTS

1 BIKE POLO 4

2 BOSSABALL 8

3 CABER TOSSING 12

4 CUP STACKING 14

5 E-SPORTS 16

6 FOOTGOLF 20

7 HURLING 24

8 OCTOPUSH 28

9 QUIDDITCH 30

10 ROLLER DERBY 34

11 RUGBY 38

12 ULTIMATE 42

GLOSSARY 46

ONLINE RESOURCES 47

MORE INFORMATION 47

INDEX 48

ABOUT THE AUTHOR 48

BIKE POLO

The world of sports goes far beyond the games seen on TV. Big sports get most of the attention, but many people play sports that aren't as well known. Take bike polo, for example. Bike polo was invented in 1891 in Ireland. Also known as "cycle polo," the game was played on a grass field. It became so popular that it was included as a demonstration sport at the 1908 Olympic Games in London, England.

Today people mostly play bike polo on a hard court, such as a parking lot or another paved surface. Hard-court bike polo was developed in Seattle in 1999. Thousands of people around the world play the sport. The game is played with teams of three or five players, and teams can be coed or all one gender. Only three players from each team are on the court at a time. Larger teams swap out their players throughout the game. A three-on-three game usually lasts 12 to 15 minutes or until one team reaches five points, whichever comes first. A five-on-five game takes 30 to 60 minutes, depending on the tournament, and uses a running clock.

Cycle polo was popular during the early to mid-1900s.

The object of bike polo is the same as in traditional polo. Players use mallets to advance a small, hard ball into the opponent's goal. They must stay on their bikes at all times. If they touch the ground with their feet, they will be considered out of play.

Most players ride with one hand on their handlebars and one hand on their mallet. They can use any type of bike, though it must adhere to league specifications. Many players customize their bikes. Most of these bikes have smaller handlebars and only one gear to make them easier to control.

Players may not touch the ground at all during the game.

BOSSABALL

Newer sports often combine the rules of more established sports to create a new game. Bossaball is a good example. Played on an inflatable, bouncy castle–style court, bossaball combines elements of soccer, volleyball, and gymnastics.

The game has rules similar to those in volleyball, with a few additions. Bossaball teams—which can be all boys, all girls, or coed—get five touches to return the ball, instead of three as in volleyball. These touches can be with the hands, feet, or head. Two to four team members pass the ball around to set up the final player in the middle. That player is bouncing on a trampoline in the center of the inflatable court.

Middle players must time their jumps off the trampoline so they can spike the ball as in volleyball or kick it as in soccer. Scoring is based on where the ball lands. Soccer kicks are worth five points if they land on the other team's trampoline or three points if they land

Players rotate around the court so that everyone gets a turn to fly high and do flips on the trampoline.

anywhere else on the court. Volleyball spikes are worth three points on the trampoline and one elsewhere.

Music is an important part of bossaball. Referees, also called the "samba referees," do not just oversee the game. They also play music, beat on percussion instruments, and entertain the crowd. During the game, they encourage players to be more adventurous in their moves.

With the aid of the trampoline, players can be creative and gymnastic in their moves.

To pass to a teammate, a player may hit the ball once with his hands or forearms or twice with any other parts of his body.

Most bossaball clubs are in Belgium and the Netherlands, but the sport has spread since Belgian Filip Eyckmans developed it in 2005. There are now bossaball tournaments all over the world. The Netherlands won the 2016 championship, which was held at the Olympic Games in Rio de Janeiro, Brazil.

CABER TOSSING

Few people can toss a caber, much less do it well. A caber is a tree trunk that can measure 18 feet (5.5 m) long and weigh 150 pounds (68 kg). At the Scottish Highland Games, not only do caber tossers pick up this enormous tree trunk; they also toss it end over end.

Competitors pick up the caber at the bottom and then walk or run forward. Once they have momentum, they stop and hurl the caber. The goal is to get the top end to land on the ground and the log to flip over straight. Competitors must be careful. If the throw is not long enough, the caber will come straight back at the tosser.

UP FOR A CHALLENGE?

Most competitions set the weight and length of the caber so that at least half of the tossers can flip it. Some competitions use a "challenge" caber that is so heavy only a few competitors can toss it.

A tosser lifts up the heavy caber and prepares to throw.

CUP STACKING

Anyone can stack cups in a pyramid. But only the best cup stackers can make three pyramids—and take them all down again—in less than two seconds.

Competitors in cup stacking tournaments start with three sets of cups that they build into pyramids. In the 3–3–3 event, players build three stacks of three cups each. In the 3–6–3 event, they build two stacks of three cups and one stack of six. In the "cycle" event, the stacker builds a 3–6–3 pattern, then two six-cup stacks, and then a 1–10–1 stack. Events are timed, with infractions given to those who do not stack in the proper order or who fumble while they stack.

People of all ages and genders participate in cup stacking. The World Sport Stacking Association tracks world records for players as young as 6 years old and as old as 60.

A competitor builds a stack of three cups and a stack of six at the 2016 Sport Stacking World Championships in Germany.

E-SPORTS

Anyone who has played a video game has played an E-Sport. Millions of people watch competitive video games. Some of the games are one-on-one tournaments. Others are team competitions. Fans watch the tournaments live in person, on the Internet, or on TV.

The most-watched games in E-Sports are team games. *Counter-Strike: Global Offensive*, *League of Legends*, *Overwatch*, and *Dota 2* all fall into this category. Teams of players—both men and women—compete against each other in tournaments all over the world. Some of these tournaments are so popular they take place in sports arenas. In 2015 The International—the biggest *Dota 2* tournament—sold out KeyArena in Seattle, Washington, in six minutes. The best team E-Sports players can make millions of dollars. *Dota 2* has the top earners, though *League of Legends* and *Counter-Strike* players follow close behind.

Team competitions are the most popular among fans.

Fans of E-Sports also follow individual games. *Street Fighter* and *Super Smash Bros. Melee* fall into this category. Players play in one-on-one knockout tournaments. Sports games such as the FIFA series of soccer video games are also played one-on-one.

THE START OF IT ALL

The first known E-Sports tournament took place in 1972 at Stanford University. The competitors played a game called *Spacewar!* First prize was a subscription to *Rolling Stone* magazine.

Two competitors in a FIFA soccer match

Reflexes and mental agility will help a player stand out from the crowd.

Because more and more people are watching E-Sports, sports leagues and TV networks are taking notice. The National Basketball Association (NBA) is a big believer in E-Sports. In 2018 it will start its own E-Sports league for NBA teams. Seventeen NBA teams will sponsor E-Sports teams to play the basketball video game *NBA 2K*. The Philadelphia 76ers own two E-Sports teams. NBA player Jeremy Lin also owns one.

FOOTGOLF

Many golfers have thought of kicking the ball instead of hitting it with a club. In FootGolf, there is no other option. In this combination of soccer and golf, players rely on leg power. Instead of needing a bag of clubs and golf balls, all the FootGolf player needs is a soccer ball—and a strong leg.

FootGolf courses are laid out on top of standard golf courses. At some golf courses, FootGolf players can play on the course at the same time as traditional golfers. At other golf courses, FootGolf players use a different set of greens. On a FootGolf course, holes are usually 75 to 100 yards (70 to 90 m) long, and sometimes up to 300 yards (275 m) long. The hole itself is approximately the width of two soccer balls. The rules are similar to the rules of golf. Players tee off at a tee box and then try to get the ball into the hole in as few kicks as possible.

FootGolf players must learn how to control their kicks so they do not overshoot the hole.

The hole is big enough to hold several soccer balls.

The game was invented in part by a professional soccer player. He and his teammates played a game in which they kicked their soccer balls back to the locker room. A friend of his translated this game into the sport of FootGolf.

It can be difficult to become skilled at golf. FootGolf, though, is easier to learn. Many players have played soccer. This helps them feel as if they are good at the game right from the start. The hardest part for these players might be putting. It is easier to kick a ball a long way than to kick it straight and slow into a cup.

Because FootGolf courses are on traditional golf courses, players must follow golf rules on dress and behavior. Since soccer is more popular than golf with young people, many golf course owners hope FootGolf might get soccer players and fans interested in traditional golf.

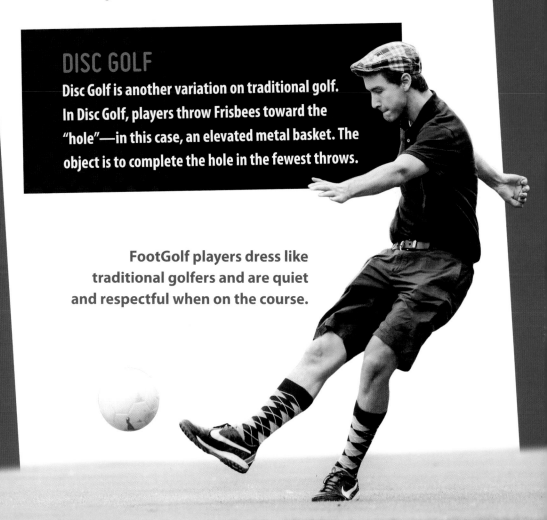

DISC GOLF
Disc Golf is another variation on traditional golf. In Disc Golf, players throw Frisbees toward the "hole"—in this case, an elevated metal basket. The object is to complete the hole in the fewest throws.

FootGolf players dress like traditional golfers and are quiet and respectful when on the course.

CHAPTER 7

HURLING

Every year more than 80,000 fans pack Croke Park in Dublin, Ireland, for the finals of the All-Ireland Senior Hurling Championship. Although hurling can best be described as the Irish version of field hockey, the sport is played all over the world.

Hurling is played on a huge field that is 150 yards (137.2 m) long and 100 yards (91.4 m) wide with H-shaped goalposts at each end. Two teams of 15 players try to get the ball, called a sliotar, into their opponent's goal. A team gets one point for hitting the sliotar between the posts and over the crossbar. A team gets three points for hitting it under the crossbar and past a goalkeeper.

Each player, called a hurler, carries a wooden stick called a hurley. The hurler uses the hurley's large rounded end to hit the sliotar. Players can hit the sliotar forward with their stick, feet, or hands. They can catch the sliotar and carry it, but not for more than four steps. The sliotar is about the size of a baseball. Usually hurlers throw it up

Players battled during a semifinal match between Cork and Waterford at the All-Ireland Senior Championship in 2017.

A LEAGUE OF THEIR OWN
Only men are hurlers. A women's version of the game, called camogie, is similar to hurling but slightly less physical.

A hurley and a sliotar

into the air and hit it with their hurley to pass to a teammate or try to score. If the sliotar is on the ground, a player can scoop it up with his stick and then hit it from waist height.

Hurlers are allowed to run into and hit each other. Their only protection is a helmet and face guard. Even the goalkeeper doesn't wear pads, but he still has to try to stop the sliotar.

OCTOPUSH

Octopush is underwater hockey played between teams of six players each. The game is a combination of hockey, water polo, and scuba diving. Players use small paddles to push a puck around the bottom of a swimming pool. Each team protects a goal at one end of the pool, and the object is to score more goals than the other team. Players are equipped with snorkels and diving fins. Even with a snorkel, most players are underwater for less than five seconds at a time. With players surfacing frequently for air, scoring a goal requires excellent teamwork.

Octopush was invented in 1954 in England by Alan Blake. He wanted to find a way for his fellow diving club members to keep busy in the winter. The first games took place between diving clubs in England. After many years, international teams got in on the act. A world championship between international teams is now held every two years.

British and New Zealand players fight for the puck during the women's final of the 2013 Underwater Hockey World Championship.

QUIDDITCH

Quidditch was conceived by author J. K. Rowling for her *Harry Potter* series. Her characters play the game on flying broomsticks. In 2005, students at Middlebury College in Vermont tried playing the fictional game in real life. They had to make up some new rules, of course, but their version of the game spread quickly.

Quidditch is played by mixed-gender teams of seven players. Players "ride" broomsticks by keeping a broom between their legs while running. Three players, known as chasers, pass a volleyball, called a quaffle, down the field. They score by throwing or kicking the quaffle through one of three hoops at the end of the field. The chasers have to get the quaffle past the keeper, who guards the hoops. A goal is worth

Chasers must get past the other team's keeper and beaters in order to score a goal.

10 points. Two players on each team, known as beaters, try to disrupt the other team's chasers. The beaters are allowed to throw dodgeballs, called bludgers, at the other players. If a player is hit, she must drop any ball she is holding and run to her team's hoops before returning to play.

After 18 minutes of game play, a neutral player runs onto the field with the snitch, a tennis ball inside a sock, tucked into his waistband. One designated player on each team, the seeker, tries to catch this runner. The seeker who pulls the snitch out of the runner's waistband earns 30 points for her team. When the snitch is captured, the game is over, and points are totaled.

More than 20 countries have national governing bodies for Quidditch. The US Quidditch Association alone has more than 175 teams. Every two years, the International Quidditch Association organizes a World Cup at which national teams compete.

Chasers can run with the quaffle, pass it to a teammate, or kick it down the field.

ROLLER DERBY

Dora the Destroyer. Babe Ruthless. Susan B. Agony. These are examples of the nicknames women in roller derby adopt. Played on a flat oval track similar to a speed-skating rink, roller derby adds a competitive component to roller skating. Matches consist of two 30-minute halves. Each half consists of several "jams," which last up to two minutes, and short breaks of 30 seconds.

Each team has five players. One player is the jammer, and the other four are blockers. Before the jam, the jammers from both teams line up behind the blockers. When the whistle blows, the jammers try to skate by the opponent's blockers. A team earns points when its jammer passes the other team's blockers during a jam.

Once a jammer has passed the other team's blockers, she skates around the track and tries to pass the blockers again. She gets one point every time she passes a blocker from the other team. The jammer who passes the other team first is called the lead jammer and can end the jam at any time within the two minutes. The lead

Blockers try to keep the other team's jammer from passing them.

jammer will try to score as many points as she can but will end the jam before the other team can score many points—or any at all.

While roller derby has been popular for decades, the modern version was developed in Austin, Texas, around 2000. It was created and managed by women, for women, though now there are also men's roller derby associations. Today, there are more than 1,500 roller derby teams and more than 400 leagues in the world.

Along with adopting fun names, players sometimes decorate their helmets and wear humorous outfits.

RUGBY

Rugby was invented in 1823 at Rugby School in England. The boys there played a game in which players could kick or catch the ball. William Webb Ellis is credited as the first boy to move the ball forward by carrying it. By 1845, boys at the school had written down the rules of their game. They distributed the rules to other schools, and rugby was born.

Today there are two major types of rugby. Rugby league is played with 13 players on each team, while rugby union is played with 15 players per side. A popular variation of rugby union, called rugby sevens, is played with shorter games and only seven players on a side. Both boys and girls play, but usually not against each other.

In all types of rugby, players advance the ball by kicking it or running it forward while their opponents try to tackle them. Players are not allowed to throw or knock the ball forward and must be

Two teams compete for possession of the ball.

strong enough to tackle opponents or break tackles while running. Players must also be able to catch and kick the ball.

Rugby league broke away from rugby union in 1895 and created a new rule for what happens after a tackle. In rugby union, players pile onto each other to compete for the ball. A team can keep the ball by winning it back after each tackle. In rugby league, the tackled player heels the ball, or kicks it backwards, and his team keeps the ball. After six tackles, the team has to kick the ball away.

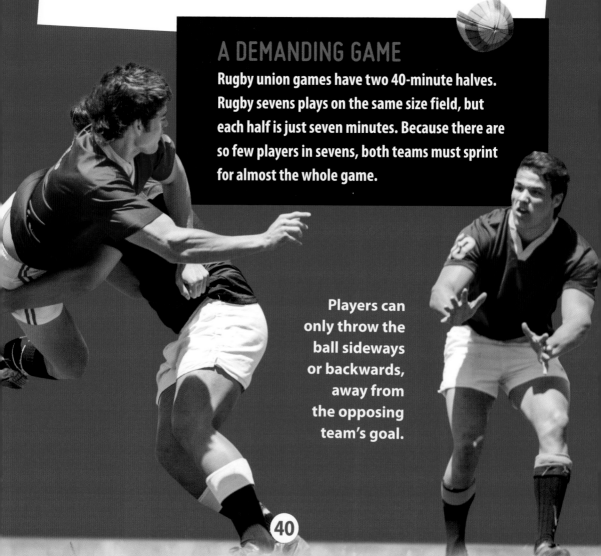

A DEMANDING GAME

Rugby union games have two 40-minute halves. Rugby sevens plays on the same size field, but each half is just seven minutes. Because there are so few players in sevens, both teams must sprint for almost the whole game.

Players can only throw the ball sideways or backwards, away from the opposing team's goal.

France tackles Ireland in the 2017 Women's Rugby World Cup.

ULTIMATE

Ultimate, sometimes called Ultimate Frisbee, combines football and basketball with the fun of tossing around a Frisbee. It is often played at schools and on college campuses. More and more people are playing in adult leagues, too.

Ultimate is played with seven people on a team. Boys and girls can be on the same team. One team starts the game by throwing the Frisbee to the other team. After catching the disc, members of the second team move the Frisbee down the field by passing the disc to one another. The player holding the Frisbee can only pivot on one foot, not run with it. He has only 10 seconds to throw the Frisbee to another player. If a player drops the Frisbee, the other team gets it. A team scores a point when one of its players catches the Frisbee in the opposing team's end zone.

Ultimate players call their own fouls. All players are asked to participate with the right spirit. This means playing fair and being honest about fouls. Although professional leagues often have

A group of players vies for the Frisbee.

After catching the disc, the player must stop running and throw it to a teammate.

referees, amateur games usually do not. These games might have an observer whose job is to help resolve disputes.

American Ultimate Disc League, the main professional league, has 24 teams all over the United States and has been around since 2012. More than 700 teams play at the collegiate level.

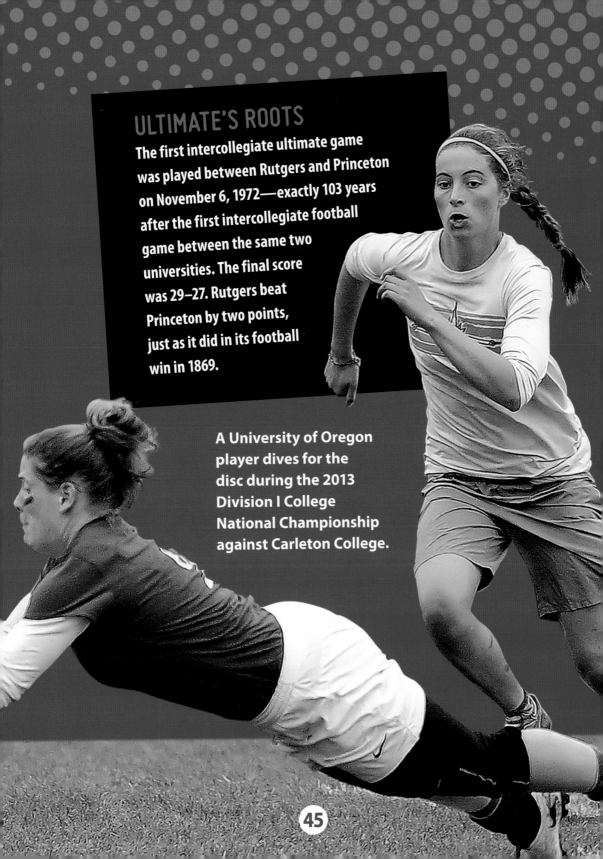

ULTIMATE'S ROOTS

The first intercollegiate ultimate game was played between Rutgers and Princeton on November 6, 1972—exactly 103 years after the first intercollegiate football game between the same two universities. The final score was 29–27. Rutgers beat Princeton by two points, just as it did in its football win in 1869.

A University of Oregon player dives for the disc during the 2013 Division I College National Championship against Carleton College.

GLOSSARY

bouncy castle

An inflatable trampoline, often shaped to look like a castle, used for recreation.

caber

An enormous tree trunk thrown in the sport of caber tossing.

Frisbee

A flying disc made by the Wham-O toy company. Since Frisbee is a brand name, ultimate players often refer to it as a "disc."

green

Where the flagstick and hole are located in golf.

jammer

A player who is trying to score points in roller derby.

knockout tournament

A style of tournament in which the winner of a match moves to the next round and the loser is eliminated.

national team

A team made up of players that are all natives or residents of the same nation.

pyramid

In cup stacking, the triangular stack of cups that a player must create.

running clock

A clock that runs continuously during timed games. The clock is stopped during timeouts; during breaks between quarters or halves; and for safety reasons, such as injuries. The clock is started again when play resumes.

sliotar

The ball used in hurling. The name is pronounced "slit-er."

snorkel

A breathing tube that allows a diver to breathe while his or her head is underwater.

tackle

In rugby, when a player brings an opposing ball carrier to the ground by wrapping his arms around him and dragging him to the ground.

tee box

The beginning of a hole in golf.

ONLINE RESOURCES

To learn more about offbeat sports, visit **abdobooklinks.com**. These links are routinely monitored and updated to provide the most current information available.

MORE INFORMATION

BOOKS

Gutman, Dan. *Sports*. New York: Harper, 2016.

National Geographic Kids. *Weird but True Sports: 300 Wacky Facts about Awesome Athletics*. Washington, DC: National Geographic, 2016.

Zweig, Eric. *Everything Sports: All the Photos, Facts, and Fun to Make You Jump!* Washington, DC: National Geographic, 2016.

INDEX

All-Ireland Senior Hurling
    Championship, 25
American Ultimate Disc
    League, 44

Belgium, 11
bike polo, 4, 6
Blake, Alan, 28
bossaball, 9–11

caber tossing, 12
camogie, 26
cup stacking, 15
cycle polo, 4

Disc Golf, 23

E-Sports, 16, 18–19
Ellis, William Webb, 39
England, 4, 28, 39

Eyckmans, Filip, 11

FootGolf, 21–23
Frisbees, 23, 42

hurling, 25–27

International Quidditch
    Association, 32
Ireland, 4, 25

Lin, Jeremy, 19

Middlebury College, 30

National Basketball
    Association (NBA), 19

octopush, 28
Olympic Games, 4, 11

Philadelphia 76ers, 19
Princeton University, 45

Quidditch, 30, 32
Quidditch Association (US),
    32

roller derby, 34, 37
Rowling, J. K., 30
rugby, 39–40
Rutgers University, 45

Scottish Highland Games, 12
Stanford University, 18

Ultimate, 42, 44–45

World Sport Stacking
    Association, 15

ABOUT THE AUTHOR

Jon Marthaler has been a freelance sportswriter for more than 10 years. He writes a weekly soccer column for the *Star Tribune* in Minneapolis, Minnesota. Jon lives in St. Paul, Minnesota, with his wife and their daughter.